The
JOHN COUGAR MELLENCAMP
Songbook

CONTENTS

TITLE	ALBUM	PAGE
A LITTLE NIGHT DANCIN'	John Cougar	9
AIN'T EVEN DONE WITH THE NIGHT	Nothin' Matters And What If It Did	17
AUTHORITY SONG	Uh-Huh	80
BETWEEN A LAUGH AND A TEAR	Scarecrow	151
CAN YOU TAKE IT	American Fool	48
CHECK IT OUT	The Lonesome Jubilee	189
CHERRY BOMB	The Lonesome Jubilee	196
CHINA GIRL	American Fool	59
CLOSE ENOUGH	American Fool	62
CRUMBLIN' DOWN	Uh-Huh	72
DANGER LIST	American Fool	42
DOWN AND OUT IN PARADISE	The Lonesome Jubilee	183
EMPTY HANDS	The Lonesome Jubilee	212
THE FACE OF THE NATION	Scarecrow	141
GOLDEN GATES	Uh-Huh	108
GRANDMA'S THEME	Scarecrow	121
HAND TO HOLD ON TO	American Fool	37
HARD TIMES FOR AN HONEST MAN	The Lonesome Jubilee	219
HOTDOGS AND HAMBURGERS	The Lonesome Jubilee	224
HURTS SO GOOD	American Fool	24
I NEED A LOVER	John Cougar	4
JACK AND DIANE	American Fool	29
JACKIE O	Uh-Huh	89

CONTENTS

TITLE	ALBUM	PAGE
JUSTICE AND INDEPENDENCE '85	Scarecrow	145
THE KIND OF FELLA I AM	Scarecrow	172
LONELY OL' NIGHT	Scarecrow	136
LOVIN' MOTHER FO YA	Uh-Huh	103
MINUTES TO MEMORIES	Scarecrow	129
PAPER IN FIRE	The Lonesome Jubilee	177
PINK HOUSES	Uh-Huh	76
PLAY GUITAR	Uh-Huh	92
RAIN ON THE SCARECROW	Scarecrow	115
THE REAL LIFE	The Lonesome Jubilee	201
R.O.C.K. IN THE U.S.A. (A SALUTE TO 60'S ROCK)	Scarecrow	166
ROOTY TOOT TOOT	The Lonesome Jubilee	233
RUMBLESEAT	Scarecrow	156
SERIOUS BUSINESS	Uh-Huh	98
SMALL PARADISE	John Cougar	13
SMALL TOWN	Scarecrow	124
THIS TIME	Nothin' Matters And What If It Did	20
THUNDERING HEARTS	American Fool	54
WARMER PLACE TO SLEEP	Uh-Huh	84
WE ARE THE PEOPLE	The Lonesome Jubilee	207
WEAKEST MOMENTS	American Fool	69
YOU'VE GOT TO STAND FOR SOMETHIN'	Scarecrow	160

I NEED A LOVER

Words and Music by
JOHN MELLENCAMP

Well, I've been walk-ing the streets___ in the eve-ning.

Rac-ing through_the hu-man jun-gles at night. ___ I'm so con-fused my mind is in-dif-f'rent.

Hey, I'm so weak, won't some-bod-y shut off that light?___

E - lec - tric - i - ty runs___ through the vi - de - o

drive me cra - zy. Some girl that knows the mean-ing of "Hey, hit the high - way."

Well, I'm not wiped out by this pool-room life I'm liv-ing. I'm gon-na quit this job and go to

school, or head back home. _____ And I'm not ask-ing to be loved _____ or be for-giv-en:

D.S. al Coda

Hey, I just can't face shak-in' in this bed-room _____ one more night _ a - lone.

A LITTLE NIGHT DANCIN'

Words and Music by
JOHN MELLENCAMP

tle,   lit - tle,   lit - tle___ night   danc - in'.

1.   G   Tacet

2.   G   G/F#   D.S.% al Coda

Coda   C   G   Em   C   D

lit - tle night danc -   in'.

Em   C   G

SMALL PARADISE

Words and Music by
JOHN MELLENCAMP

Repeat and fade

Small par - a - dise...

small par - a - dise.

AIN'T EVEN DONE WITH THE NIGHT

Words and Music by
JOHN MELLENCAMP

THIS TIME

Words and Music by
JOHN MELLENCAMP

This time — I think I'm real - ly in love. —

real - ly in love. —

I hope you don't lose that in - no - cent

laugh - ter,

hope time does - n't take that a - way. —

D.S. 𝄋 *and fade*

HURTS SO GOOD

Words and Music by
JOHN MELLENCAMP and GEORGE GREEN

28

JACK AND DIANE

Words and Music by
JOHN MELLENCAMP

two A-mer-i-can kids grow-in' up in the heart-land.

Jack, he's gon-na be_____ a

foot-ball star;_____ Di - ane deb-u-

tante back seat of Jack-y's car.

Jack, he says, "Hey, Di - ane, let's run off be -
"Well, then, there, Di - ane, we got - ta

hind a shad - y tree; _____ drib - ble off those
run off to___ the cit - y." Di - ane says,

Bob - bie Brooks. Let me do what I please." Say - in',
"Ba - by, you ain't miss - in' a thing." But Jack, he says,

Oh yeah, ___ life goes___ on, _____

Oh, let it rock, let it roll. _____

Let the Bi - ble belt come and save my soul. _____

two A-mer-i-can kids do-in' the

Repeat and fade

best that they___ can.

HAND TO HOLD ON TO

Words and Music by
JOHN MELLENCAMP

DANGER LIST

Words and Music by
JOHN MELLENCAMP
and LARRY CRANE

CAN YOU TAKE IT

Words and Music by
JOHN MELLENCAMP

take it all the way down?___ Can you real - ly take it all ___

___ the way down, down,___ down? ___

Down, down,___ down. ___ So we watch a lit - tle

T V, I drink up the fam - i - ly wine.___

THUNDERING HEARTS

Words and Music by
JOHN MELLENCAMP
and GEORGE GREEN

CHINA GIRL

Words and Music by
JOE NEW and JEFF SILBAR

It's been my good for-tune to find you, Chi - na girl.

Stol - en

Repeat and fade

CLOSE ENOUGH

Words and Music by
JOHN MELLENCAMP

WEAKEST MOMENTS

Words and Music by
JOHN MELLENCAMP

CRUMBLIN' DOWN

Words and Music by
JOHN MELLENCAMP
and GEORGE GREEN

PINK HOUSES

Words and Music by
JOHN MELLENCAMP

AUTHORITY SONG

Words and Music by
JOHN MELLENCAMP

I call___   I say oh___

___ no_____ no no.___ I say oh___ no_____

no no.___ I say oh___ no_____   no___ no no._____ I___

D. S. 𝄋 and fade

WARMER PLACE TO SLEEP

Words and Music by
JOHN MELLENCAMP
and GEORGE GREEN

I need to find a warm-er place to sleep.

Well, I

D. S. % (no repeats) al Coda ⊕

Coda

find __ a warm-er place to

Repeat and fade

sleep. I need to find a warm-er place to

JACKIE O

Words and Music by
JOHN MELLENCAMP
and JOHN PRINE

PLAY GUITAR

Words and Music by
JOHN MELLENCAMP,
LARRY CRANE and DAN ROSS

You may drive a - round your town in a
got your eye on the cheer - lead - er queen and you're

brand - new shin - y car; your face in the wind, and your hair - cut's in, and your
walk - in' her home from school. You know that she's on - ly sev - en - teen, but she

friends think you're bi - zarre.
knows that you're a fool.
You may find a cush - y job,___ and I
You know you can't touch that stuff___ with - out

hope that you___ go far.
mon - ey or a brand - new car.
But if you real - ly want to taste some cool suc - cess, you
Let me give you some good ad - vice, young man: you

bet - ter learn to play gui - tar.___
bet - ter learn to play gui - tar.___ } Play gui - tar,___

play gui - tar,___ play gui - tar. _____
Play gui -

tar,_____ play gui - tar,_____ play gui - tar. _____

1.

2.

You

All wom - en a - round the world____ want a pho - ny rock star

Tacet

who plays gui - tar. _____

No chord

SERIOUS BUSINESS

Words and Music by
JOHN MELLENCAMP

LOVIN' MOTHER FO YA

Words and Music by
JOHN MELLENCAMP
and WILL CARY

suck-in' moth-er fo ya, don't you know.__

Squeeze me, girl, don't let me fall.__ I wan-na walk, don't want to crawl. Make me feel__ like a

GOLDEN GATES

Words and Music by
JOHN MELLENCAMP

know to   be true   are the prom - is - es   made from   the   heart._____   Just the

prom - is - es   made from   the   heart.

RAIN ON THE SCARECROW

Words and Music by
JOHN MELLENCAMP and GEORGE M. GREEN

Rain on the scare - crow, blood on the plow. Rain on the scare - crow,

blood on the plow. The crops we grew___ last sum - mer___ were - n't e -

nough to pay the loans,___ could - n't buy the seed___ to plant this spring and the

Farm-ers Bank fore-closed. Called my old friend, Schep-man, up to auc - tion off the land; he said,

GRANDMA'S THEME

Traditional
Arrangement by
JOHN MELLENCAMP

SMALL TOWN

Words and Music by
JOHN MELLENCAMP

Got noth-ing a-gainst a big ___ town,

still hay-seed e-nough to say "Look who's in the big town." But my bed ___ is in a small ___

___ town; oh, and that's good e - nough ___ for me. _____

MINUTES TO MEMORIES

Words and Music by
JOHN MELLENCAMP and GEORGE M. GREEN

On a Grey-hound thir-ty miles___ be-yond James-town,
The rain hit the old dog in the twi-light's last gleam-ing,

he saw the sun set on the Ten-nes-see line. He looked at the young man who was
he said "Son, it sounds like rat-tling old bones. This high-way is long but I

You are young_and you __ are the fu - ture, so suck it up_ and tough it out, and

be the best_ you can. __

The old man had a vi-sion but it was hard for me to fol - low,

I do things my way and I pay a high_ price._ When I think back on the

LONELY OL' NIGHT

Words and Music by
JOHN MELLENCAMP

She calls me up and says, "Ba - by, it's a lone - ly ol' night."
Ra - di - o play - in' soft - ly some sing - er's sad, sad song.

I don't know, ___ I'm just so scared ___ and lone-ly all at ___
He's sing-in' a-bout stand-in' in the shad-ows of love. ___ I guess he feels ___

___ the same time. ___
aw-f'lly a - lone. ___

No - bod - y told us it was
She says, "I know ex -

gon - na work out ___ this way, _____ no no no no no. ___
act - ly what ___ he means, _____ yeah yeah yeah yeah yeah." ___

THE FACE OF THE NATION

Words and Music by
JOHN MELLENCAMP

more. And the face of the na - tion keeps

chang - in' and chang - in'. The face of the na - tion, I don't

rec - og - nize__ it no more. Face of the na - tion.

Hey, face of the na - tion. Face of the na -

JUSTICE AND INDEPENDENCE '85

Words and Music by
JOHN MELLENCAMP

He was born on the fourth day of Ju - ly____
Na - tion grew up____

so his par - ents called him In - de - pen - dence Day.
and got him - self a big rep - u - ta - tion.

BETWEEN A LAUGH AND A TEAR

Words and Music by
JOHN MELLENCAMP

When par - a - dise__ is no long - er fit for you to live in
When this__ card - board town can no long - er a - muse you,

RUMBLESEAT

Words and Music by
JOHN MELLENCAMP

1. All _____ the leaves are green; all _____ my friends are gone; I'm
2. 3. (see additional lyrics)

liv-in' in my home-town; I can bare-ly get a-long. I feel sor-ry for my-self; that's an

Yeah, we'll go___
Yes, I'll blow___

Hey!

2. Well, I could have a nervous breakdown,
   But I don't believe in shrinks;
   I should be drunker than a monkey
   But I don't like to drink.
   Call up some girls,
   But I'm afraid of the phone;
   I'm always talkin' to myself;
   I guess I'm never alone.
   Am I the only one that feels this way?
   I'd buy myself some stylish clothes;
   But I sure hate to pay.

   Chorus

3. The sun is coming up;
   Just goin' to bed.
   I combed my hair with my pillow;
   Still got some dreams left.
   Tomorrow is a new day;
   Gonna make these dreams come true.
   I'm gonna believe in myself;
   I'll tell you what I'm gonna do,
   I'm gonna stop puttin' myself down;
   I'm gonna turn my life around.

YOU'VE GOT TO STAND FOR SOMETHIN'

Words and Music by
JOHN MELLENCAMP

I've seen the Roll - in' Stones,__ for - got__ a - bout
ki - ta Krush - chev kiss - in'

R.O.C.K. IN THE U.S.A.
(A Salute to 60's Rock)

Words and Music by
JOHN MELLENCAMP

THE KIND OF FELLA I AM

Words and Music by
JOHN MELLENCAMP

Well, I don't like it when I see your eyes dart-in' back ___ and forth a-cross the room ___

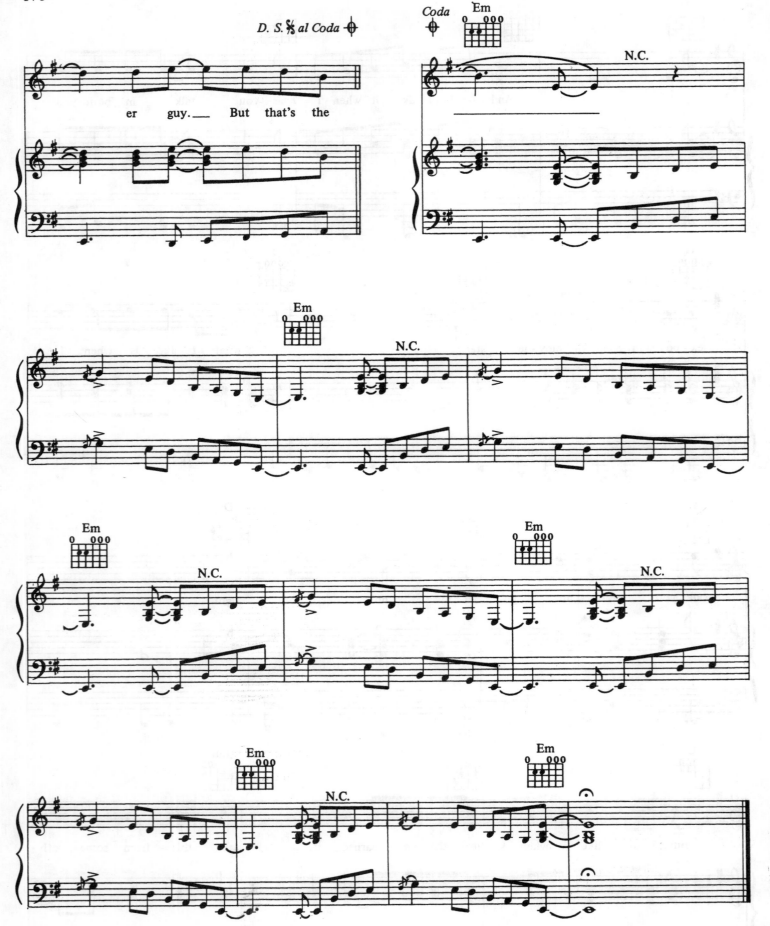

PAPER IN FIRE

Words and Music by
JOHN MELLENCAMP

DOWN AND OUT IN PARADISE

Words and Music by
JOHN MELLENCAMP

CHECK IT OUT

Words and Music by
JOHN MELLENCAMP

A mill - ion young po - ets_
A mill - ion young po - ets_

all that we've learned a-bout hap - pi - ness.

(Check it out.) For-got to say hel-lo to my neigh-

CHERRY BOMB

Words and Music by
JOHN MELLENCAMP

200

THE REAL LIFE

Words and Music by
JOHN MELLENCAMP

1. Su - zanne— div - orced— her hus - band, she got the keys to the car— and the home..
2. Jack - son Jack - son was — a good kid; he had four years of col - lege and a bach -
3. *See additional lyric*

I want the real life.___ I want to live___ the real life."___

Additional lyric

I guess it don't matter how old you are,
Or how old one lives to be.
I guess it boils down to what we did with our lives.
And how we deal with our own destinies.
But, something happens when you reach a certain age,
Particularly to those ones that are young at heart.
It's a lonely proposition when you realize
That there's less days in front of the horse
Than riding in the back of this cart.
I say:

Coda (chorus)

WE ARE THE PEOPLE

Words and Music by
JOHN MELLENCAMP

Medium Rock

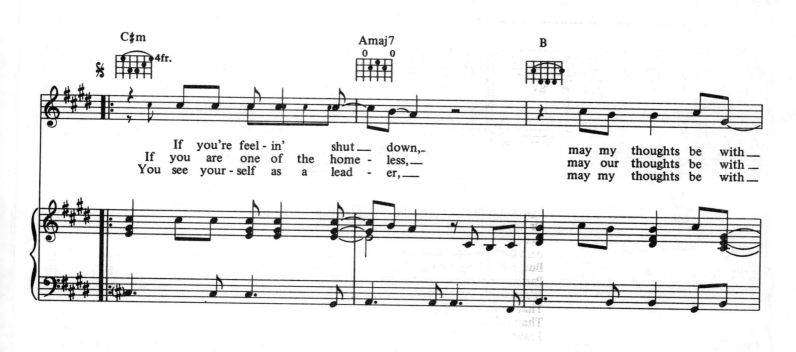

If you're feel - in' shut __ down, __ may my thoughts be with __
If you are one of the home - less, __ may our thoughts be with __
You see your - self as a lead - er, __ may my thoughts be with __

EMPTY HANDS

Words and Music by
JOHN MELLENCAMP and GEORGE M. GREEN

There's_ too man-y peo-ple with emp-ty hands.

HARD TIMES FOR AN HONEST MAN

Words and Music by
JOHN MELLENCAMP

HOTDOGS AND HAMBURGERS

Words and Music by
JOHN MELLENCAMP

Dri-vin' down,— on a dry— sum-mer's day, old Route—

Six - ty Six,___ and I___ was just___ a kid.

Met a pret - ty lit - tle In - dian girl___ a - long___ the way. Got her in -

to my car___ and tried to give her a kiss. "I'll give you

beads and wam-pum, what - ev - er it takes, girl,___ to make you trade." She

jumped in - to the back seat and she kind - a flipped_ her lid. She said, "You're try - in' to get

some - thing for noth - ing like the Pil - grims in the old - en days."_

We rode for a-while till the sun went a - way and I re-

giv - in' up__ or hold - in' on.__

So I dropped her off at some rail-road cross-ing in Tex-as; an old

In - di - an man ___ was wait - ing there. ___

He smiled and thanked me, but he saw right through me. ___ I could tell he did-n't

like - me; for my kind he did not care.

ROOTY TOOT TOOT

Words and Music by
JOHN MELLENCAMP

lot of peo - ple out there who are at the end of their rope."

Some - times, ba - by, you've got to lay low. Root -

y toot toot, root - y toot toot, we had it made in the shade, like a

ball through the hoop. Spin-nin' and tum - blin' in - side this hoo - la hoop.

made in the shade,___ like a ball through the hoop___

Spin - nin' and tum - blin' in - side___ this hoo - la hoop.

Liv - in' and learn - in', root - y toot toot.

N.C.